WOLF PACK VS. MOOSE

BY NATH...

BELLWETHER MEDIA • MINNEAPOLIS, MN

TM

Torque brims with excitement
perfect for thrill-seekers of all kinds.
Discover daring survival skills, explore
uncharted worlds, and marvel at mighty
engines and extreme sports. In *Torque* books,
anything can happen. Are you ready?

Library of Congress Cataloging-in-Publication Data

Names: Sommer, Nathan, author.
Title: Wolf pack vs. moose / Nathan Sommer.
Other titles: Wolf pack versus moose | Animal battles (Bellwether Media)
Description: Minneapolis, MN : Bellwether Media, 2021. | Series: Torque.
  Animal battles | Includes bibliographical references and index. |
  Audience: Ages 7-12. | Audience: Grades 4-6. | Summary: "Amazing
  photography accompanies engaging information about the fighting
  capabilities of wolf packs and moose. The combination of high-interest
  subject matter and light text is intended for students in grades 3
  through 7"– Provided by publisher.
Identifiers: LCCN 2020003034 (print) | LCCN 2020003035 (ebook) | ISBN
  9781644872833 (library binding) | ISBN 9781681037462 (ebook)
Subjects: LCSH: Wolves–Juvenile literature. | Moose–Juvenile literature.
  | Predation (Biology)–Juvenile literature.
Classification: LCC QL737.C22 S664 2021 (print) | LCC QL737.C22 (ebook) |
  DDC 599.773–dc23
LC record available at https://lccn.loc.gov/2020003034
LC ebook record available at https://lccn.loc.gov/2020003035

Editor: Kieran Downs   Designer: Andrea Schneider

Printed in the United States of America, North Mankato, MN.

TABLE OF CONTENTS

THE COMPETITORS

Frozen **climates** are home to strong animals. Moose have **adapted** to survive these climates. The **agile** giants are built to last in tough **habitats**.

Hungry wolf packs often challenge moose. With strength in numbers, wolves do not fear the moose's size. Who is the champion when these beasts face off?

Moose are the largest members of the deer family. They have humped shoulders, powerful legs, and long **muzzles**. Hairy, saggy skin called a bell hangs from their necks.

Moose only live in areas with **seasonal** snow. The giants roam forests in northern Asia, Europe, and North America. They prefer to live near lakes and ponds.

STRONG SWIMMERS

Moose are great swimmers. They can hold their breath for almost one minute when diving for food.

BELL

MOOSE PROFILE

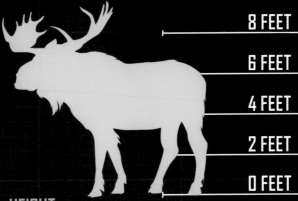

8 FEET

6 FEET

4 FEET

2 FEET

0 FEET

HEIGHT
UP TO 7 FEET
(2.1 METERS)
AT THE SHOULDER

WEIGHT
UP TO 1,323 POUNDS
(600 KILOGRAMS)

HABITAT

FORESTS

WOODLANDS

SWAMPS

MOOSE RANGE

■ RANGE

7

GRAY WOLF PROFILE

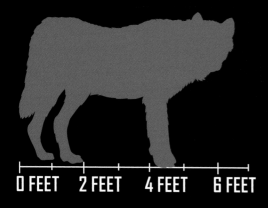

LENGTH
UP TO 6.6 FEET
(2 METERS)

0 FEET 2 FEET 4 FEET 6 FEET

WEIGHT
UP TO 130 POUNDS
(59 KILOGRAMS)

HABITAT

WOODLANDS

PLAINS

DESERTS

TUNDRA

GRAY WOLF RANGE

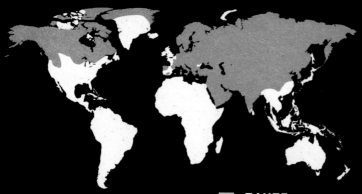

RANGE

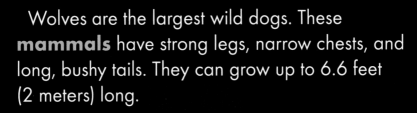

Wolves are the largest wild dogs. These **mammals** have strong legs, narrow chests, and long, bushy tails. They can grow up to 6.6 feet (2 meters) long.

Wolves are smart, highly social creatures. They live and hunt in packs of around 10 wolves. This makes them **apex predators** in almost all habitats.

PACKS ON THE MOVE

Wolf packs will go to great lengths to find food. Some travel over 50 miles

SECRET WEAPONS

ANTLERS

Male moose are crowned with an impressive weapon. Their **antlers** can reach up to 6 feet (1.8 meters) across! Male moose use them to

Wolves fight as a team. Communication and teamwork help them outsmart and defeat much larger animals. Howls call packs to fight. Growls scare off enemies.

SMART COMMUNICATORS

Wolves also talk to each other through their actions. They show teeth, tuck back their ears, and move their tails to show how they feel.

Long legs help moose reach speeds of 35 miles (56.3 kilometers) per hour. Their legs are also used as a weapon. Powerful kicks can instantly take down enemies.

MOOSE SPEED

TOP MOOSE RUNNING SPEED
35 MPH (56 KM/H)

TOP HUMAN RUNNING SPEED
28 MPH (45 KM/H)

WOLF

LARGE PACKS

ENERGY

SHARP TEETH

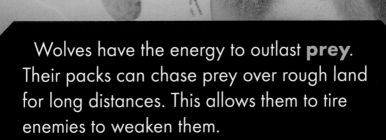

Wolves have the energy to outlast **prey**. Their packs can chase prey over rough land for long distances. This allows them to tire enemies to weaken them.

SECRET WEAPONS

LARGE ANTLERS

LONG LEGS

HOOVES

Hooves help moose balance on soft ground. They give moose a quick escape over snow. Moose also use their hooves to stomp enemies.

**2.5 INCHES
(6.4 CENTIMETERS)
LONG**

Wolves have razor-sharp **canine teeth**. Powerful jaws sink these teeth into prey with hundreds of pounds of **pressure**. The teeth can cut through thick skin, fur, and even bone!

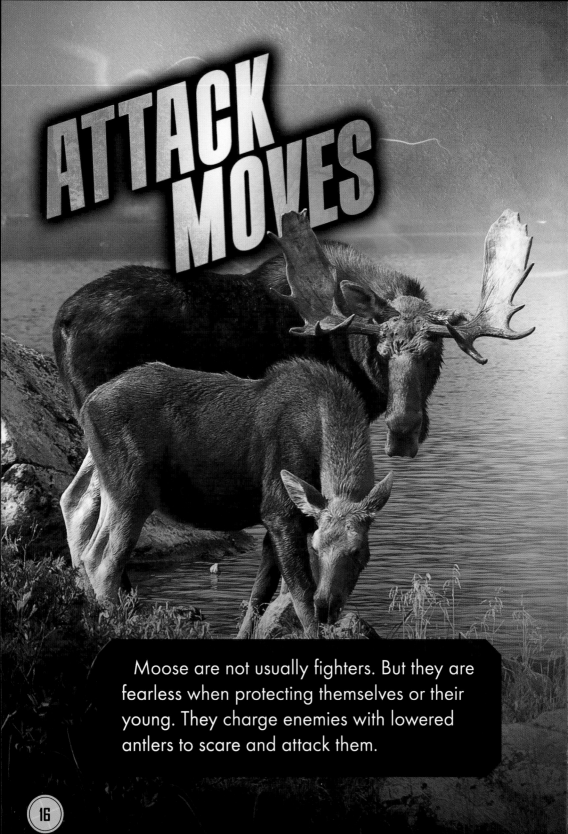

ATTACK MOVES

Moose are not usually fighters. But they are fearless when protecting themselves or their young. They charge enemies with lowered antlers to scare and attack them.

Wolves team up to outnumber enemies. One wolf spotting prey may bark to warn the entire pack. The pack then circles their enemy and stops them from escaping!

SUPER SENSES

Wolves have sharp senses. They can smell animals more than 1 mile (1.6 kilometers) away and can hear miles into the distance.

Moose attack if their **scare tactics** fail.
Forceful blows from their legs wound enemies.
They then stomp weakened attackers with their

Wolves attack as a pack. Multiple bites from several wolves quickly take down prey. Packs stick around to eat every piece of what remains!

READY, FIGHT!

A mother moose is circled by three wolves. The smaller wolves bite the moose's nose as the **alpha** jumps on its back.

The moose slams the alpha to the ground and kicks it. The alpha is defeated instantly! The moose stomps a smaller wolf as the third runs away. This giant cannot be outnumbered today!

GLOSSARY

adapted—changed over a long period of time

agile—able to move quickly and easily

alpha—the leader of the wolf pack, usually the strongest male

antlers—branched bones on the heads of some animals; antlers look like horns.

apex predators—animals at the top of the food chain that are not preyed upon by other animals

canine teeth—long, pointed teeth that are often the sharpest in the mouth

climates—the specific weather conditions for certain areas

habitats—the homes or areas where animals prefer to live

hooves—hard coverings that protect some animal's feet

mammals—warm-blooded animals that have backbones and feed their young milk

muzzles—the noses and mouths of some animals

pressure—the amount of power or force placed onto something

prey—animals that are hunted by other animals for food

scare tactics—a fighting strategy in which one animal tries to make itself appear as large or scary as possible in hopes of scaring the other off

seasonal—relating to a certain time of year

TO LEARN MORE

AT THE LIBRARY

Herrington, Lisa M. *Gray Wolves.* New York, N.Y.: Children's Press, 2019.

Sommer, Nathan. *Grizzly Bear vs. Wolf Pack.* Minneapolis, Minn.: Bellwether Media, 2020.

Winnick, Nick. *Moose.* New York, N.Y.: Smartbook Media Inc., 2017.

ON THE WEB

FACTSURFER

Factsurfer.com gives you a safe, fun way to find more information.

1. Go to www.factsurfer.com

2. Enter "wolf pack vs. moose" into the search box and click Q.

3. Select your book cover to see a list of related content.

INDEX